Loss Adjuster

*For Roger and Anne,
with all best
wishes*

*David Ashbee
St. James Church
Dursley
14-6-2008.*

Published by bluechrome publishing 2007

2 4 6 8 10 9 7 5 3 1

First published in Great Britain in 2007 by
bluechrome publishing
PO Box 109,
Portishead, Bristol. BS20 7ZJ

www.bluechrome.co.uk

A CIP catalogue record for this book is available from the British
Library

ISBN   1-904781-57-8
        978-1-904781-57-8

Printed by Biddles Ltd, King's Lynn, Norfolk

Loss Adjuster

David Ashbee

Dedications

This collection is dedicated to all family members and friends mentioned in the poems, especially those in *The Cherington Poets*, whose inspiration I have relied heavily on for over 15 years, and in *The Cheltenham Poetry Society*, who have helped me to decide what worked.

Acknowledgements

The author wishes to thank the editors of the following magazines in whose pages several of these poems first appeared :

Rialto; *Smiths Knoll*; *Envoi*; *South*; Edge Festival and Cheltenham Festival anthologies.

Also thanks to the organisers and judges of these competitions for prizes and commendations:

Envoi 133 for "Ash" (3rd. Prize); *Blinking Eye* for "Shelley"; Yorkshire Open for "Four Eggs"; Ware Poets 2004 for "After Hermione left"; Cheltenham Poetry Society for "Environmental Health" (1st. Prize) and "Cockerels among cabins."

All of these poems were initially written to be read in isolation without reference to each other. In grouping them here into a sectioned sequence, it is hoped that extra resonance will result.

However, the consistency of persona across the whole cannot be assumed. While much of the material is autobiographical, many details, scenes and perspectives are fictional, ludic or satirical.

Contents

Warning | 13
Here is One of Me | 15
Loss | 16
Loss Adjuster | 17
In the dark | 18
Edie | 19
Hungry | 21
All the Fun | 23
Last Coin | 24
Winner takes all | 25
Fathers - a triptych | 26
Still the ticket | 29
Back to the S & D. | 31
I think I hear it coming | 32
Between Marriage and Divorce | 34
"System restore" | 37
Old cine-camera | 38
First flash | 40
Education | 41
I have fought thistles | 42
Special Edition | 44
Betrayal | 45
Tongs | 46
The gale | 47
The Duel | 49
Dolphin House | 50
Four Eggs | 51
Those Moments | 52
Camera Obscura | 53
Piano | 55
Balloons | 57
Balloon and holly | 59
Torn | 61
The Shirt | 63
His hat | 65
Removal | 66

Don't believe the forecast 68
Antiques Warehouse 69
The Dreamer 73
Miracle 75
Skipper 77
Spring-cleaning the Woods 79
The Collector 80
Skateboarders 81
"Miss La La at the Cirque Fernando" 82
Siphoning the Sump 83
Steven 85
Gloucester 1990 89
Bishop Hooper 90
Ivor Gurney hoeing at Sandhurst, June 1922 91
Ivor Gurney and the dog 92
Gurney's River 94
River Voices 95
Arlingham 96
The Trans-sexual River 97
"Forty Acres" 99
Welcome Street 100
Ballad of The Beast 103
Pay per view 106
Fur flies 108
The Black Pad 109
Chap in a balaclava? 110
Interrogation 111
In Memoriam Cecil Giddings 1899-1989 115
School Boxing Match 117
Still Talking to Bob 118
For Roger 119
Questions 120
Eleventh of November 121
Environmental Health 122
Ash 124
Homage to Eddie 125
On the 30th Anniversary of Elvis Presley's death 126
Homage to Stanley 127

Farewell O'Grady 128
After Hermione left … 130
The absence of front doors 133
Ghost Walk 135
Horreos 137
Hostages to Fortune 138
From a Bangkok Boarding House Noticeboard 139
Cockerels among cabins 140
Shelley 141
Three flies 142
Last Fly 143
Last glimpse 145
This Moment 147
"A Final Word from our Leader" 148
The Leader 150
Déjà vu 151

Loss Adjuster

Warning

Do not throw stones at this poem.
There is no charge
for reading it, but the bull
in your mind's china shop
cannot read and may
charge himself.

No refunds given. The management
cannot be held
to ransom.

The ideas in this poem
may settle after packing.
Do not imbibe the gel.
Dispose of in a safe place.

Nothing of value
is kept in this poem overnight.
We give no credit, meaning
not to offend.

Use the green box provided
to recycle old lines.
We cannot go on burying
our dead.
Unruly metaphors will be asked to leave
or pulped as cliché.

If you need insight,
don't take ours.

The stanzas are not vehicles
for bumping and boring
but for dodging.
Please respect other traditions
moving in the vicinity.
Beware of the tattooed man
in the red stanza
and of bright sparks overhead.

Waiting limited, return
prohibited.
In the event of misunderstanding,
stay with us to the end.
There is no hard shoulder.

This poem goes one way only.
No exit permitted through the cafeteria.

Whether you think this is fair or not
you are bound to be right.

If you can read this
you are too darned close.

The next two pages
are deliberately left blank.

Your comments will be posted on our website.

Here is One of Me

Here is one of me
in a garden one Bank Holiday.
I took it when I wasn't looking.

The garden was a temporary refuge,
a place I bought when desperate.
It was all right for lounging between dandelions
in the small hours before tea.

This here is a dog I bought on impulse
for a son I bought on impulse
but who is never in
to look after the dog.

The trouble with catching yourself
unawares like this
is that you've never tidied up.
Nor did I notice the sun had gone in.

This next one I took with more panache.
It's the sun-lounger cooling under black clouds,
while the wind billows its canvas,
destroying the imprint my body left
when I had gone in.

Here is one of me writing a poem.
It's not very good.

Loss

Do you know that feeling
of reaching into your pocket
as you've done each Friday night for years,
to grasp the folded note
that buys the round

and find there's nothing there,
not even
a fluff-filled corner of the lining,

just an inch-wide hole
through which you touch your thigh?

Now imagine a hole
that your whole life's slipped through,

when every day for weeks
you rummage through a vacancy
you still can't grasp is true.

And every day for years
you wonder
at what turn in the road,
which shrug of the shoulders
did the trick,

unwound the thread
that looped the latch
that sprung the trap
she slipped through.

Loss Adjuster

It took me half my life to realise
I was a born loss adjuster.

People seeing me at wrecks and disasters
assume I am a ghoul.

But there's money in these bent fenders,
oil patches, fragments of skin.

You can't put a price on a life, they say.
But I must barcode everything.

You have to, when your name's on a list
and folk have expectations.

Sometimes I'm given a discreet *carte blanche*
when the family aren't at home.

Early morning is the best time
before the scavengers come.

Adjusting loss is an acquired knack.
Most men are too sensitive.

I do retain a squeamish side
But I pull myself together and *get on.*

In the dark

I've found something,
here, in the cavity's dark
but can't say what it is.
Only fingers fax it to my brain
in a half-familiar tongue.
I might as well be in an iron lung,
an encased mummy reaching for a cat
and finding only teeth
or wet flinchy eyeball.

It may be just a party-game to you
but for me this is *it* –
pushing past a curtain with outstretched hand
in a minefield of spikes
amid the camouflage of branches.

Each knob I grasp and turn could
detonate
or win me the jackpot,
pouring milled coins at my feet in an earthquake clatter.

Bull in a china shop, that's what I am,
though I flutter meek as a moth
among dented empty cans,
at any time expecting
the crack of a ball on the back
of my coconut skull.

Edie

It was two white cats that fused the memory,
or more the gloom behind them,
stark dimensions of a simple room
like drapes,
framed in a window from the street.

A chain unravelled fifty years.
Here was the house of the whiskered woman
whose skin was a paste of dirt,
the house no neighbour entered ;
a house of shouts and musty silences,
its curtains drawn on a summer's afternoon.

The man was boldest – he might fling *"Hello"*
if I had dared it ,
as he trudged up the gateless path
to the peeling door.
The other woman – his wife ? - I can't recall.

But Edie was seen about.
Wrinkled stockings and battered shoes,
wreathed feet that scuffed and stumbled.
Saliva glistened on the hairs around her mouth,
a toothless mouth that sagged
like a dead frog.

She was always served first at the chip-shop,
while the queue shrank in itself, and feigned
an interest in adverts
for *Fleur de Lys* pies, tubs of potatoes,
the bus like a spaceship passing in the night.
Hardly was her back turned
when out came a cloth -
to swab the counter down.

I didn't see the fire,
didn't even hear the clanging bell,
the shouts as bulky men slid ladders up,
just saw the blackened walls,
the windows more inscrutable than ever.

They must have been rehoused,
the trudging man, his shadow-wife,
and the boy who went to a different school
whom no-one dared to fight.
As for Edie's ashes
I was too young to enquire.

Hungry

In boyhood streets at eleven o'clock
the only place alight
was the corner chip-shop
gasping its fatty breath to dew
the blue tobacco night.

My fingerprints dissolved on tin
as I stretched until my toes ached
to watch the corpulent magician
stoke his hissing engine
and fan his boiling lake.

Chips spilled like gravel from his scoop,
fillets sizzled on the hot-plate
or slapped wet on the slab,
while from the draughty lean-to at the back
came the thud of stripped potatoes.

Beguiled by his patter, how patiently we queued
for his shovelled gold and scattered juices,
admired his wife's deft origami
as she folded and moulded
the salt-spattered last week's news.

Taller now, I lean across the counter,
hoping in vain for fabulous tales
from this temple of the night.
But its handmaids, swathed in green and orange
to match the menu-board and tiles

are sullen and ill-at-ease with talk.
They process plain white packets
through a digital machine,
while a tall chap, trimmed for business,
approves each hygienic act.

Standing before the Perspex hatch
I feel my palate cloy
at alien shapes of Jumbo Hot-dogs,
veggie-pancakes, ribs in curry sauce —
relishing only the Real McCoy.

And I feel a rising hunger
that this studded slimline boy
and his schoolgirl servers in their natty hats
could not begin to recognise,
no matter satisfy.

All the Fun

What went on
in the pooled light
where coconuts thumbed their noses
and goldfish hung in bags
was all a game.

And just a game
that dodging and weaving
as the bent tin sparked
and the tattooed man
must have dropped your change.

The real stuff
went on behind the canvas
where mud gave way to grass
and shapes too big for dogs
shrank from the light.

Rock'n'roll
was barking in your ear
like a sergeant-major
when looking up you saw
the flashing panel of names

Bob Beryl Bill Betty

But your pockets are empty
and tomorrow they'll be gone.

Last Coin

I remember rolling my last thin coin,
a poor boy at the fair,
and can still smart at that final loss
now, as it touches you.

I understand your quivering lip
when the carousel horse slows down,
and your urge to thump and smash
those cheating slot-machines.

However it comes, it hurts,
the unavoidable grief
that lurks in a handful of pennies
soon frittered away.

What after all
are money-boxes for,
those well-fed pigs
and grinning chimpanzees ?

Should we say
"Easy come and go"
like some we know,
who never make it last?

Eduardo, for instance,
who shrugged and laughed
across his well-mopped plate
then moved abroad to a fresh start,

having tossed his past
like a coin soon lost.
How it must sweeten life
to never reckon the cost.

Winner takes all

Rich boys hoarded them in a bag
with drawstrings, like a dap-bag
sewn by their mothers.

Poor boys kept them in their coats –
a risky thing, for poor boys' coats
soon run to holes.

Derek kept his in a tin,
an *"Erinmore"* tin that his uncle left
when he went off to war.

The currency of our back-streets,
they juddered over cobbles
and leapt across the kerb,

where the gutter-drains,
with their iron ribs
and ever-open jaws

would snap them up
like a croc snapped up
the sailor in *"The Wizard"*

and pocketed them,
a silver plop in the black depths.
laughing *"Winner takes all."*

dap - regional vernacular for plimsoll or pump

Fathers - a triptych

I.

When Father papered the parlour
he set the scene for the rest of our days.
Not only fern-leaves at calculated angles
but a maroon-squiggle border
and three ducks that could never fly away.

Daddy's Sauce on the table
and during the TV rugby too.
"Don, not in front of the children."
Eternal father who saved
shillings for the meter, screws in a tin,

I saw you today in an old magazine
when we took up the carpet,
secure in your armchair doing the Pools,
your walking-stick in the umbrella stand,
black brogues by the hearth.

It didn't really hit me you had gone
until the Father's Day Parade
when they all turned up in foreign cars
with their shaved heads and ear-studs,
and you weren't there.

There isn't a parlour to paper any more,
just one through room with a vinyl floor,
the piano still plays - on a DVD,
and there's a plasma screen where your ducks used to be.

II

Wait 'til your father gets home
he used to hear some mothers say,
swiping their offspring's bony legs
and dragging them away.

His mother never said it once,
that threat or promise she couldn't make true,
just got on uncomplaining
with what she had to do:

digging potatoes, darning stockings,
working a six-day week to pay
for Christmas, shirts and blazer,
their seaside holiday.

She raised him well, her sudden son,
and launched him into life,
never dreaming one day he'd make
someone a lovely wife.

III

The son is father to the man,
and here he is, astride the miniature train
as it poops around the figure-of-eight,
clutching him against the fall.

They wave for my camcorder
that tracks them with obsessive eye
as they clatter over bridges, points,
to disappear through trees.

When he returns him to his mother
it cuts him to the quick.
Sunday night's not good
for a weekend dad,
a better dad than I ever was,
than I ever had.

Still the ticket

At 18 he frisked the wayside stations
for yellowing handbills,
parcel-slips for junctions long defunct,
pasteboard tickets from a vanished era
in mottled blue or striped maroon.

And what he found,
out where their platforms ended
and tracks converged in grass
past ramshackle carriage-sheds
towards derricks and gantries
on alien horizons,

what blew against him there
with the brittle leaves,
the smell of refineries'
sludge-thickened lakes,
was his first sense of remoteness.

Now at 60, when remoteness
is marketed in oils,
he sees from a briefly stopping train
how towers have mushroomed all around
and wayside platforms
crumbling in his memory
are tarmac drives to industrial estates.

It's just for a moment,
bridging a single line
that still performs some purpose in a crisis
as it curves away through unmolested acres,
that he knows he wasn't crazy after all,
that a derelict world
is somehow whole again.

Back to the S & D.

The pit villages of North Somerset
are drenched with evening rain,
the Mendips grey with a mist-shroud.

Paulton Baptist Church,
the chipshop in Hallatrow,
these sanctify the twilight.

I cannot raise the heart for Temple Cloud.

Between blue steel leisure centres
and the padlocked compounds
of industrial estates,
the cycle-path is swallowed
by dripping conifers.

Midsomer Norton's spoil-tip
glistens with runnels.
Soaked in drops, it
burps in its blackshirt sleep.

This is the land
of the long-gone Summer Folk,
the trackway of the dawdling
Slow and Dirty.

I think I hear it coming

Sheltering from the rain
beneath the enormous arch
where thistle and willowherb
thrive all around

(It is an offence to go beyond this point)

or leaning on the parapet
of Staffordshire blue brick
above a trackbed
throttled by saplings

(Drivers must seek permission to proceed)

facing the fenced-off darkness,
admiring the ornateness
of this mouth into the hill

(Do not lean out of the window)

I think I hear it coming

The bark from its brass-ringed chimney
its scalding oatmeal steam
its joggers' elbows pumping
its fists punching *yes yes yes*

its bulk and roar as it
bears down upon me.

I step back down the bank

One
two
three red carriages
lolloping, lolloping
almost empty
apart from a seated silhouette
and the guard who waves
as if I'm really there

and it pants into the distance
as the rain sweeps down
pattering the leaves
making the lane's gravel glisten.

The sky brightens.
I walk the rough track
to the stationmaster's house
where a metal milepost
in the middle of the lawn
says how far it used to be
but not how far I've come.

Between Marriage and Divorce

While I was married, this is what they did:
demolished the engine-shed,
and built brick boxes on the sidings site
where newlyweds could live.

We'd moved to the country.

The sheets on the lines were soiled with smuts.
smelt of a smoke you can't get now
for love nor money.

Today I passed the demolished shed.
What shed ? they said.
There's nothing there.

But I can hear its hissing
everywhere.

System Restore

"System restore"

The screen says : *"Select a date."*
I'd love to but
they're all married or dead,
grown mad or lumpy.

"June," I choose .
There's one available.
"Enter".
And the figures ripple
like clothes coming off.
Can time be so strippable-down?

I wait what they call *"a moment."*
Everything will be done for me.
Flesh falls off in folds
and here I am, back
in the Garden of Eden ,
when systems were pure and unvirused.

Whatever was bugging me seems to be cured.
My commands are brisk and athletic.
I can pick, scan
and have it.

Whatever you lost can be yours again
with *"System Restore."*

Old cine-camera

Don't know if they do it now
except on DVD's
when life's too fast to catch
and the eyes fill with water.

But my old cine-camera
with those picture strips
you could hold up to the light
and find to your bewilderment
that nearly every moment was the same
and you had to walk miles
to find any difference —
but we were used to walking then —

my old cine-camera
would run films backwards on the screen.

There's the family kitten
flying up to the top of a wall,
paws uncannily finding the brick
and landing like a party trick.

There is me in hippy stag-night gear
backing into the lavatory
while unzipping my flies.

There's my best man, still alive, and slimmer,
standing at the wheelhouse in a lock
while the water-level falls
and spouts of water cascade up the sluices,
making Newton a lying fool.

There's the filly I failed to back
obligingly retreating down the track
before the white post at The Curragh.

There are you and your father, arm in arm,
making your way serenely
in a dead march
back up the church path,
your smile fading to nervousness
as you duck into the ribboned limousine.

Stop it ! Stop it there !
Look! That's me,
still standing at the porch door,
the rest of my life behind me.

First flash

That such a concrete land-locked ship
should become a wooden barque!
That scabby-kneed boys could sit in awe,
sherbet-dabbed fingers poised unlicked
as Caliban comes snarling in
from the Green Room near the fish-stall!

That crabbed cane-wielding teachers
should have heart to transport us to
an enchanted isle at the city's core!

I didn't take much detail in at 10 :
shaken-sheet-metal thunder
in a strutting patchwork pantomime
was enough to cast a spell.

Was it Antonio I saw in after years,
striding long-legged into town up Southgate?
Often I meant to stop and ask but didn't,
in case he was a mirage or impostor,
unable to face his embarrassing blank stare,
the notion that they'd vanished into air,
that student-mariner rabble,
leaving no beach-wet footprint in St Michael's Square.

Those rogues and clowns could all be dead,
that Prospero a heap of cast-off buskins,
and all their wooden O a realm of ash
who slashed those cartoon visions on the brain
of a schoolboy blinded, jolted into knowledge
by a thunderclap, that first life-changing flash.

Education

Before *"Othello"*, that most black-and-white of plays,
I first encountered Avon's sights and sounds,
saw how a reed like a woman's body sways,
how Iago-esque the river's glare confounds
a knot of branches, makes the quick mind leap
to twist askew the blue sky's sleight of hand.
And I understood what fruit the heart can reap
from a stem-glass balcony's one-night stand.

But I also recall the sniggers, and the state
we left the coach in, stopping off for chips ;
the tight-jumpered girl I lingered at the gate with,
longing for a favour from those Cupid-bow lips.
At fourteen, Stratford taught me all of this,
how eternal is betrayal with a kiss.

I have fought thistles

Once, with a machete, fork and gloves,
juveniles that easily came round
to my way of thinking.

Once with a scythe.
I'd never swung a scythe before.
but all night long I felt like Marvell
whose glow-worms lit my dreams.

But for my first fight
when I earned my spurs
I used a sword.

I was twelve years old.
The sword was rusty but it did the job.
Taken with permission from a friend's uncle's barn.

The place was Shurdington.
Someone since must have done it better
for the place is tidy now
with farm-shops, smart new houses,
and a junction to the M5,

While anyone who lets small boys
take sharp blades to slash unwatched through fields
would wrap himself in headlines.

Me? Real swords?
It was no dream, believe me .
But fields were different then.

Was it swinging a sword
or vanquishing thistles
that I think made me a man?

Or the chance
they gave us then
to get blood on our hands?

Special Edition

No room in the hall
so I kept it propped at the wall
by the bay-window.

Not locked. For who would nick
a scratched, black
pre-war carrier-bike?

Almost a penny-farthing
with that small front-wheel,
ideal for steering.
.
It weaved a treat through rush-hour buses,
even with a hundred rushes
of the day's news.

But I never took a chance again
with that slip-knotted string.
Once was enough.

They mobbed and mocked
like gulls, those *City Final* pages,
as they dived under cars like scalded cocks.

I got most of them back,
their Stop-Press with the latest odds from Epsom
franked by tyres or dog-muck.

The most obscene example of that
gutter-press fell on the mat
at 20 Carlton Crescent

where the light was never on
and they left the cash with their neighbour
twice a month.

Betrayal

The day the boards went up
I sat on the stairs with him
and waited for the knock.

One last thing to be done,
like handing over keys
or reading the meter.

He seemed surprised when I
grabbed him. Don't think I'd
bothered to feed him. No point.

Small for his age, and soft.
He went in so quietly.
No scratching, no mews.

A creak as they strapped the lid.
His eyes, twin torches,
burned behind the wicker.

It gets to me now, but hindsight's tricky.
In those days I'd have sent
my Granny to the wall.

Tongs

I will now consider the gift of tongs.

Not neat sprung ones for a sugar-lump,
but clasped hunkers with crab-claws
to grapple with coal.

I used to hold you tight,
raised you, and placed you
on the furnace of the bed.

Now only ashes
lace the cold grille.
My clutch is empty.

If I were to make you
a gift of tongs,
what should you think?

Would you remember the baskets I filled,
the fires I heaped,
or think of hard and grasping fingers –

the pressure needed to keep hold?

The gale

Canvas billowing above my head
and I snug in a sleeping-bag
when I saw your shadow,
heard your footsteps squishing in wet grass
as the guyropes tightened.

You seemed to have panicked as you often did.
Did what you must.
Whether I got up at all
to join you in that cold dark field
I can't remember
but I slipped back into sleep.

You say you lay awake for hours,
taut and trembling with the tent
while I snored on,
my part in it done.

Harsh morning light showed the damage :
the campsite like a stubblefield
with what could well have been body-bags
lumpen in the grass.

I've heard your version once,
though you weren't one for recriminations,
and sometimes got things wrong.
Like Horatio you kept the bridge,
kept the whole frame standing.

Do you recall we tried to straighten
those bow-legged poles,
and marvelled how mere wind
could warp them so?

Meanwhile, out in the Atlantic,
the yachts were limping home,
ragged as scarecrows and
grateful for their lives.

At the time I felt we were survivors.

The Duel

"Arguments could fill a marriage like water, running through everything, always, with no taste or colour, but lots of noise."
                        – Barbara Kingsolver, "Prodigal Summer"

We had water-pistols.
Kept out of sight in the main, but sometimes fired.

I kept mine in the pantry with the empties.
Never found out where she kept hers.

I remember how they cut the skin
with their cold lasers.

When I squeezed the trigger, I'd be annoyed
by my wet hands.

But it was fun while it lasted, which was not long.
Those stains on our clothes soon dried.

One hissing squirt, and – look!
"Of course they're not tears."

We both had a licence. Doesn't everyone?
Shotguns are another matter.

Dolphin House

was going for a song
but the song of the dolphin is an unknown tongue

a Georgian gentleman's residence
between tannery and a takeaway

had a brass knob and a dolphin knocker
that a yob knocked off with a brick

a garden that reached to a stream
and no way over the wall beyond

so many rooms you could lose yourself in
and we did

a gazebo in the garden where I slept
most often when she started throwing things.

Four Eggs

"Four eggs!" I sang
like an anthem,
bearing them in triumph
through the kitchen door,

as if this daily roll-call
from the bedded straw
gave shape to our
disintegrating days.

You looked away.

I perched them in the rack,
pleased how neat they sat,
but one teetered,
rollocked across my foot

and cracked on the floor.

"Three eggs!" I called
as if the next stop down the line.

Coiling slimy fragments
in a tissue to the bin,
I thought it worth
a warm new-laid egg

to have seen spread
across your face,
like yolk,
an unforced smile.

Those Moments

Last week, by the lake, the cloud-strewn scene
changed so fast on the looming mountains
that the brush had barely time to mix
before the spotlight swung elsewhere.

Today, in the office, everyone looked up,
left their screens and lifted blind-slats,
longed for lenses to capture
that rare glow on the hills.

In the grey of a sudden evening,
I trudged through rush-hour crowds,
up dingy stairs to a lawyer's rooms
to sign and seal last papers.

Returning home, I felt a calm,
the pulse not racing like those leaves
that fear the blast and cower in gutters,
sensing times have turned.

On a day when mauve skies clearing
made a foil for the bracken aflame,
only a girl on the radio
sounded, for a moment, like you.

Camera Obscura

Up the renovated tower
through a smell of damp plaster
past empty paint-tins, sanded wood,
until we reach the gallery.

"Shut the door. It must be dark."
So dark we cannot see
each other's face
as we turn the handle and pass on.

Each unwinds in a slow pavanne
until the movement is complete,
all the while peering
as the world unfolds.

Look! There's someone could be you,
gazing gull-like from the bridge,
face drenched with silver light
that the distant mud-bank throws.

And look! There's me, but older,
prodding with a stick across
the Downs' unravelling green.
Where will it end?

Everything moving.
Trees, traffic, buildings,
pouring through this funnel
in a waterfall of sky.

I can't see your face
or hear your heart,
but here we are on both sides,
swaying round the corkscrew of our lives,

a Moebius ribbon
that drops our dilemmas
back at our feet
like a pleased retriever.

I didn't think to fly
so far in one cramped room,
shoulder to shoulder with strangers
round a spinning bowl.

And when we descend,
slowly, in a daze,
there, in her booth, is the woman
like a fortune-telling gypsy.

Can she guess what we have seen?
All of us who thank her
and step out blinking
to a strangely new city.

Piano

Sad old house
where a piano plays
late into the night.

A languid tune
that leaks through sashes,
casements' sulphur light,

drifts over the gardens'
withered leaves and walls
of broken stone.

I own no part
of these moon-thrown shadows,
have outgrown

the musty taste
of sour laments
and bluish ivory airs

once borne in long-lost
lumbering journeys
over shores and streets and stairs

from other cities,
more frenetic days.
How it stutters to pronounce

the exactitudes of
its off-key chords
and brine-soaked sounds

across a gulf so wide
I cannot bridge or reach
or imagine how.

Let it play.
I could be touched,
but it doesn't touch me now.

Balloons

Was it balloons I saw?
On a day too late for carnivals,
that ripened yellow
as a plate of pears.

Three of them at least,
red ones, swooping
up the slope like children
eager to be free.

Not a sudden shower —
a basket of pigeons
shaken and fizzed — but a
flung bolas, a pawnbroker's sign.

Feeling like a snail,
home heavy on my back
and love a burden,
I had slipped the leash

to drive without desire
over crossroads, through villages,
past golf-links, quarries,
twisting unsignposted lanes

into feelings lost for a dozen years
and stumbled on again
among tangled woods with muddy paths
below a monument.

Here, spread thin as oil
to a misty horizon,
yellow-silver distances ran clear
like stored wine.

Fall in the valley
had opened new vistas
through which the breezes came
ruffling, searching

and caught me up,
a glider on the thermals,
over roofs, fields, hills,
and, somewhere lost, the river.

Suddenly – balloons!
glimpsed only for a moment,
swept away from a huddle
of cement-rendered houses,

torn from a child's grasp
or a spray of celebration,
a bough of apples shaken free
by wild September.

They melted,
as liquid as they grew,
seeding the hopes they rode upon
like baubles of the air.

So much sky to vanish into.
So much air
to drink and drown against.
So much to let go.

Balloon and holly

("As the saucer reminds us of the cup,
the things that are not mentioned
will go on existing." - Robert Rehder)

Just as an empty saucer proffers a cup
whose weight can set your hand trembling
tinkling the spoon
and tilting liquid that could scorch your throat,

so the blue balloon I saw
wedged against the holly hedge
grew beyond Still Life.

A skin sphere, swelled to bursting,
and the point itself – one keen angle
on a curled leaf –
almost touch in a neat geometry.

This case has caught my breath before.

Our infant son released his tight-clutched globe,
entrusted to the air that red fat wonder,
and watched in awe as it swept away,
twitching its label like a tail.

We didn't win the Distance Prize.
Home-sick perhaps, or trapped by circumstance,
it snagged on a holly-tree
that towered unreachable from a sheer bank
as four mouths gaped below.

Disaster primed to happen.

Again, years later, mute with trepidation,
I thought to save our floundering balloon.
But its dancing days were over
and my attempts at rescue foiled
by her prickly phrase : *"Too late."*

Not just scenes, but a whole life unravels
as you clutch an empty saucer,
watch a balloon go up.

All down the street I listened for the bang.

Torn

I tore up my room by the roots.
The mat of dead flowers was too demeaning.
No time for measures or sensible planning.

With armchairs upended,
dust-clogged mementoes were smashed, unregretted
as I tore my room up by the roots.

Outside was all wet snow.
No nest here for a mat of withered flowers
with its decade of stains.

So I drove it to the salvage tip,
hurled it into an iron skip
among oil-cans, sad rags, the wreckage of gardens.

This was not the weekend pilgrimage
when everyone I've ever known
queues up as at an altar-rail

to jettison their dead,
joking as the caskets of a wasted life
are shipped away.

This was a lonely bone-yard.
No smoke rose from the chimney
of the one man left in charge

who picked his way through the wheel-grooved slush
in his world of mist and icy water
to check I was okay.

I left my mat of flowers among his souvenirs
as he stood by rusty fridges, blowing on his hands
and watched me drive away.

Back home the room was dry and vacant
like a ballroom after hours,
shivering in its coat of grit and hairs.

Only the mirror remained intact.
At its open door a red-cheeked stranger
watched what I would do.

The Shirt

My father owned this shirt.
The felon who stole it from his washing-line
was caught and shot.
I wear it as a tribute to my father's
no-nonsense approach,
and to the thief's bravura.

A well-known former correspondent
for the *BBC's World Service*
sports a poor imitation,
a sort that could be bought some years ago
in the markets of Bangkok.

My father personally
supervised its laundering
He checked the water temperature,
insisted on a certain hand-made soap
and always ironed it himself.

Envy of this shirt
contributed to my mother's end.
In a scribbled death-note
pinned to the summer-house door,
she referred obliquely to my father's rage
when he found it left out in the rain.

After his own death, it was thrown away
by a superstitious maid.
Imagine my euphoria at finding it
in a locker at a downtown lido.
God knows how it got there.

I feel *right* in it,
though it is, I confess, conspicuous
with its embroidery of peacocks
and gold-thread epaulettes.

That, of course, was all some years ago –
before Gasparo Mendes
immortalised it in an opera
which ran and ran.

And then I had my breakdown.

Thanks to regression therapy
I no longer rely on
tokens of my past.

Tomorrow I auction the shirt
for a hospice charity.

His hat

He wore a sort of globe around his head ;
on its grey felt ocean, an archipelago
of places he had been –
Paris, Amsterdam, Oberammergau.
One day, when they all joined up
and he plucked it from its peg,
he'd have the whole world in his hands.
He would be Atlas, heading this ball in
for the winning goal in the World Cup.
But the wind came in with a tackle
and robbed him in the midfield.

Now he drives an eight-year-old *Montego*
with *"We've seen the lions of Longleat"* on the back.

Removal

Not the ideal day,
when October damp in August
turns the beechwoods on the hill above
to a rain-forest
and we're stripped to the waist
as we unscrew wardrobes,
manhandle sofas down the slippery lawn
and pause a lot for fruit-juice.

Spiders startled by sudden daylight
skitter off like the house's ghosts
until it's all too transparent
how frail are the shells we live in.

That's when *she* arrives.

All her resentment
at this frank dismantling
tips the darts she fires.

He should have hired a second truck.
Never considers anyone but himself.
Has he offered anyone tea?

And as he makes himself scarce,
sorting timber-lengths in the garage,
she spits out bits he never told me —
wonders why she gave him thirty years.

But there they are – the doughnuts,
coffee on a tray,
and warm sausage-rolls.

This is what she's good at :
from the unravelling threads
of a house shorn like a traitor,
she magics a feast,
an excuse to ease protesting limbs
and sit around on whatever's at hand
casually reminiscing –

as if, instead of this messy taking-down,
we were builders of the eleventh hour
setting roofs, foundations.

As in a way we are.

Don't believe the forecast

I promised them Elysian fields
but over-rated the forecast.

How could I explain, as we huddled in the drizzle,
what it was I'd seen

the purple mountains fold on fold
the waving meadows starred with gold.

"Don't start that again," they said
as if they didn't ever hum the tune,
"now what about that inn?"

I'd promised them a special place for afters,
The Adam and Eve at Paradise.
I know it sounds unlikely but
it's the sort of place you stumble on round here.

Yes it was there, and begging for business –
managed by a repentant fallen angel,
a *Green Dragon Enterprise Inn.*

I won't say they forgave me
when I bought the first round
but even chilled-to-buggery
Bonkbuster Ale has its uses
for unclogging teeth of stale bread.

We've broken bread together often since,
determined to remain active
if not exactly friends.

Antiques Warehouse

What is it they want, these people who lack nothing
but come here mooching, every wet weekend?

They'll know when they see it – something not expensive,
dear only to the heart, that stubborn fickle bidder.

Something they'd forgotten ever was, lost long ago in linings
of cast-off clothing sent for refugees.

Something even Mother was embarrassed by,
always kept wrapped in a lavendered drawer.

recalling now the eerie way the light had
of hovering on empty afternoons

above the shepherd on the sideboard in the parlour,
the woodland scene in cracked oils on the stairs.

Something to restore what they failed to inherit
and fill that space beside their double-bed,

something to match, or amazingly to open
that vexing box for which they've lost the key.

Cast List

The Dreamer

(for Tricia and Mike Henry)

Local legend has it that if you sleep on the mountain, your dreams will come true.

1.

The dreamer came striding back at dawn,
shrugging off the mountain behind him,
trailing clouds of knowing
that shrank to rags of nimbus
in the frost-blue sky.

We fretted for his revelations,
 this traveller from a bracken bourne,
but all he sought was porridge,
then coffee and the gas-fire,
the brittle shell of home.

2.

The dreamer has no care for dreams.
It was waking on a mountain that he sought,

to see how words might coalesce
like dew beneath the dawn,

then rise to the druid shapes of cromlechs,
runic symbols on the page.

3.

The strident voice of the dreamer's wife
rises from the room below.
Reciting? — Or is she cross?

I imagine the dreamer
hungry for sleep,
hunched in his chair.

Through the window looms
the shadow of the mountain.

Miracle

(for Barry Cox)

By no stretch is he a twitcher.
Just the kind of guy who keeps
a bird-book by his window,
and lays on more exotic feasts
for his jolly feathered playmates
than he ever does for himself.

A humdrum garden,
but autumn tufts and leaf mould grubs
have the same appeal for birds
as salvage tips for totters.

See him at his window now,
struggling with the knurled wheel
of his catalogue binoculars,
frustrated that all they show him
is a spiny gut of shrub.

Too close to focus.
So it's back to the naked eye,
naked until he nudges those bifocals.

And it's still there.
A miracle!
God's on his side and a stranger
has honoured him with a visit
to whatever that bush is called.

He takes a long look. Prurient,
he feels, this gazing to memorize
vital statistics.
Eye-liner, beak-shape, rump.

There's a chart in the back of his book
that soon sorts out the fledglings from the boys,
the dipper from the golden oriole.

But some birds haven't read it.
Fashions come and go like whitethroats.
This one matches nothing
that S.M.Fotheringale, R.A.
has caught in vivid oils.

It's the pale stripe on the forehead
foxes him. A bush-bunting but
the measurements are wrong.
This is almost wren-size.
And he's not blessed with its song.

The need to identify frets him.
Perhaps a newer more comprehensive guide
with his birthday token.
But the image in his head will vanish
in a few days. Or become confused.
This he knows too well.

All those nights browsing by the lamp
while the woodburner sighs and crackles,
hoping to unpeel a sticky page
and fall upon its portrait,
like that of some lost apostle

exactly as he thinks it was
years after
when the garden's laid to concrete
and his eyes don't see too well
and the milkman won't bring bottles any more.

Skipper

He was my top lad that day.

After the pratting and the backchat,
his play-to-the-gallery smirk
when he could turn the girls against me with
a dismissive flick of his quiff,

he had put up his hand like a raw rookie
and said the magic phrase *"I will."*

It wasn't him at all.
When the rest were burbling in the wings
and needed hushing,
dousing with cold water like randy dogs,

he was growing paler,
more intense.

The winners of the Minors Cup –
mere sprogs –
came off to huge applause,
grinning like Bruce Forsyths.
One of them was his younger sister's heartthrob.

He couldn't muster that gift of tongues.

"Sir, do you mind if we
run it through again.
In the car-park outside.
Not in here."
This was true grit.

But his opening quotation slipped and fell flat in the wet.
His second phrase wheezed like a clogged harmonica.
John Wayne, hogtied.

"I'm sorry, I just can't do it.
I feel sick."

And he was.

By the time the Intermediate team came on,
he was ringing his dad for a lift.

Now, here he is, running out,
the Skipper for Saracens' Thirds,
spring-heeled, punching the air.

Much more his thing.

Spring-cleaning the Woods

Now the travellers are back on the road
or holed up somewhere else,
beautifying some picnic-spot or layby
with their laundry and Alsatians,
Keith is mopping up their mess.

The glade in the centre, where four paths meet,
is a stock-car starting lineup.
A burnt-out *Toyota*, a *Fiesta* shell,
and legless hunchbacks blotched with rust
squat ready for the tip.

"A change from logs," grunts Keith,
grinning through his Green Man fungus
as he jumps from the cab of his pick-up
whose chain-winch dangles like a gibbet.
"If I had my way, these buggers…"

Not all travellers' cast-offs by a long chalk.
He saw two boy-racers leg it,
their pea-green *Lada* wedged against a beech.
As he'd spun the wheels to haul it pathwards,
sparks flew, and he'd sweated.

Once, the smoke that curled up from these woods
was a hermit's, brewing char or squirrel stew.
Keith would have trekked with axe on shoulder, whistling.
Now he bawls from his pick-up when he spots them:
"You bloody sods. If I get 'old of you …"

The Collector

I'm waiting in Bull Pitch (for Micky to finish his bath),
perched in the early-morning sun
on one of those thigh-high curved-top walls
from which the railings have been sawn,
leaving handy knobs to hook the dog-lead on.

This is what it's all about. No rush.
Time to watch the town spill by.
Some toddle, some nod, some look at a list
as if I'm a nut or a mugger.

Behind me, in Number Nine, a plughole glugs,
the front-yard drain froths briefly.
I select a key from the bunch
and mount the echoing staircase.

Standing at his bedsit door,
with a towel wrapped round like a sultan in a sauna,
dripping onto the lino,
Micky counts out the fivers.

Skateboarders

Hip art this
if hip's not too dated
for this understated cool.

Soon as school's folded
they're back,
working at flips and twists
in churchyard and precinct,
from ramp or speed-hump
soaring up like *Harriers*,
a metre nearer the moon
a moment only, until
smack!
they hit tarmac with a
crack that scatters cats.

The pigeons that wheely-hop the slabs
have given ground
to these patchwork jackdaws
with their neck-jerk promenading
going for the burn with
alley ballet.

Their buskin garb is baggy and patched,
obligatory and shabby
the branded baseball caps.

Rattling good stuff their poetry,
lyrical in snatches,
their dialect garbled,
mono
syllabic
as rap.

"Miss La La at the Cirque Fernando"

(another poem about family life)
(for Jen)

She likes to get the bit between her teeth
or rather she likes to be seen
the way she hangs
by the skin of her teeth
awaiting her due of applause,

but more than this
she likes to release the bit,
falling to land nimbly on her feet,
hoping they notice her butterfly-trembling,
the momentary whiteness of panic fading
to the flush of exertion
before, again,
applause.

Without this she would not feel whole
when, loosed of all ribbons,
the constrictions of elastic,
she sprawls, like a corpse
fished out of the harbour
gasping :

"I can't bear it,
I can't bear to go on"
- her other nightly performance.

Siphoning the Sump

(For Alice)

Outside her door is a sump,
a concrete-slabbed pit in which rainwater gathers.
To drain it is a weekly chore
in Perigord summers
when showers, like Bergerac Sec,
sizzle in the sun-bleached grass
and trickle down this concrete throat
in sweet libations.

But today we launched The Ark.
The drip of the tap in the sink
became a gargle in the gutters
and soon under apricot boughs
the straw-flecked lane was a glinting beck.

The sump-level lapped at the kitchen door,
a sky-transfer mock-up of the village lake
we had planned to picnic by,
which lay freckled and grey through the weeping trees.

The hose, an orange snake, lay bedded in washed gravel.
She'd shown me the trick some years before.
A physics lesson in Perigord Vert.
Sluice the hose with water from the tap,
then plunge it, thumbed, into the brimming sump.

But I lacked the knack.
Down the cowhoof-dappled lane
the open snout trickled,
like old Percy at the porcelain,
then gurgled dry.

That's when it occurred.

Stepping out in her tangerine mules,
she slipped, zip,
on the slick board over the cesspit,
and sat there,
ass in wet cowshit,
a rowing-boat beached in a herring-bone stream.

Now she prowls the house in a Chinese gown,
hoovering up, like a spider,
the shrivelled wings of flies,
while the hosepipe lies in the puddled lane abandoned,
its silver gullet gaping to be fed.

Steven

With a Citroen's chug,
a gravel crunch and a cork-pop,
Steven's back
from wherever he has been.

No ears for his dry one-liners now.
We are busy regaling ourselves
with *"The Barley Mow"*
in four different keys.

He stands in the lamplight,
brown as a local,
bemused.
This is not his scene.

Much later, when I wake at 3 a.m.
a slit of light
edges underneath his door
like a postcard.

A Current Under Slabs

Gloucester 1990

This city has,
as Calvino says they all have,
a certain lost grace —
seen only when a pallid winter sunlight
plays on its face.

An alley opens
jaws of broken teeth
and smiles away regret
as sunbeams' probes reveal
an open green beyond,
and a statue's silhouette.

From the back stairs of the *Barton Stores,*
an almost lost perspective
springs to view,
between the top floor (closed by the recession)
and the loo.

From here, you see the bypass
leapfrog miles of sidings
to the meadows,
and hills whose shoulders ripple
mauve, lime or amber
as clouds play tag with their shadows.

Bishop Hooper

One of the half-timbered buildings to survive
the clean sweep of the Fifties
was called Bishop Hooper's Lodging .
Lodging seemed an odd thing for a Bishop
but the phrase stuck.
Now it housed his stake :
glass-cased in the Folk Museum,
a round chopping-block, grooved and charred.
At ten a boy's drawn to such things.
This riddled chunk took pride of place
from the Old Spot sow and model barquentine.
The musty smell of creaking attic rooms
with northlight glossing the floorboards
had always worked their magic.
Now I could sniff the incense on his robes
and a strong whiff of burning
Then I found his statue.
Behind the cathedral he waited for me,
patient in his stone cage.
Was it a blessing his hands performed
or did he warm them in the flames?

I'm no believer. Got no faith,
not even that soapsud wishful-thinking
that lumps leyliners with the crystal crew.
But Bishop Hooper cuts the mustard.
John Hooper had what it takes,
the bottle it needs to say to a hard-faced woman:
"No dice. I'll take the fire."

Ivor Gurney hoeing at Sandhurst, June 1922

"Awfully hot today, the hoeing most slow.
aghast at such a waste of weeds,
quite unable to help hacking the corn."

"It's not far from the river : two meadows."
And there above them stands Gloucester Cathedral,
her tower agleam in the June morning.

In the next field, a horse and plough
prepares the ground for more promising seed
than this harvest he reaps, a tangle of thorn.

"A lovely brown thing, with noble furrows
that come straight up. The farmers are nice indeed,"
he wrote. And then the feared, the forlorn

note: *"The verses are rejected wholesale."* So.
"Carnegie is done with." Wherever the path leads
next is uncertain. But there are warning

signs. The brown river's glide. This field he hoes,
the way the midday sun pricks the beads
of sweat from skin the thistles have torn.

"Awfully hot today, the hoeing most slow.
aghast at such a waste of weeds,
quite unable to help hacking the corn."

Ivor Gurney and the dog

(for Ann and Andrew Kennet)

"I'll take my dog and my airgun too
And I will take a ramble" - *Glo'shire travellers' song*

From Stone House, Dartford, Kent,
pained by licks of lightning
that set ablaze his blankets,
he scribbled pleas on yellow sheets,
the grounds on which he sought release,
having *"really injured none."*

"Took a dog out for walks (for kindness);
saved it from eating, kept its health,
and sometimes beat it,
but was kind to it."

In this photo, from 1922,
the poet basks in Westfield Terrace,
a Jack Russell on his knee.
Sunlight falls on solid steps of stone.
Behind him, uncarpeted stairs
lead up to darkness.

Why does he bark so much
and chase his tail?
Is there a storm coming
that no-one else can sense,
electrical tricks from the sky?

Or is he just undisciplined,
desperate to run free
through Twigworth trees and stoney brooks
to Severn meadows?

But no regime or rope could hope
to curb such liberty.
The theme recurs in chords, off-key :
"Beat a dog,
for kindness."

Gurney's River

How Gurney's Twyver changed!

Not always the map's kingfisher flash,
the brook that sang and quenched him
through meadows south of Maisemore,
where Sandhurst elver-scoopers stalked
with mesh-nets strung on poles.

But a current under slabs
on his boyhood route to school,
the Roman's stream that channelled
the hardcore of the hills
to fortify Glevum,
buttress abbey-walls,

a silver wash across city streets
from the cattle-market pump,

or the lower stretch, an open ditch
full of tanyard washings,
thick with lime and fat
the year that he was born,

that made its sluggish way
past the vinegar factory
where Deans disdained to walk

to disgorge its stinking cargo
of cans and shoes and cats
beside the ruined priory
in the now-defunct "Old Severn,"

the blocked route to the sea.

River Voices

'Er's late.
The more as comes from Bernigum
The more er kips um waitin'

They sez to me
"That ent ten foot 'igh."
"If it wuz,"I tells um,
"I wouldn't be stood yur!"

They gets it off the telly,
but it means ten foot on the Sharpness gauge.
Thur wuz a time when the local rag
never allowed fer the clocks goin' on.

I suppose it's all trade for *"The Anchor"*
but it's like a ruddy theme park.
I likes to see it lash out at um
on the bank at Stonebench,
then drown their fancy cars.

Surfboards, they'm OK
if they knows what they'm at,
but motor-boats be damned,
shouldn't be allowed.
They've no respect whatsoever. It's
like shooting Moby Dick.

Arlingham

They say there was once a ferry here
where muscular Tom Phillips
fireman-hoisted ladies through the mud.

A whistle to the farther shore would bring him,
rolling athwart the current,
or twisting, a barely-moving insect,
where no water seems.

Plums, timber, chicken – even oxen –
were hauled across the wind-peaked surges,
delivered safe through his huge hands.

Those days are gone. Stinking mud
has long since globbed the pits of his waders.

Where standard-furling Roman legions forded,
a shelf of rock is sometimes seen
rippling the low-tide shallows:
a rope-bridge of sandbanks
twists a slippery noose for fools.

Newnham's russet chest against The Forest
seems another country in the haze;
sometimes a gleaming tray-stacked toytown
an infant's clutch away.

Only the indolent or pensive come here now,
drawn to drink or gaze,
lacking the courage or the hunger
the drove simpler men to walk on waves.

Between us, time's insidious river
sluices hidden channels, throws up sand,
blurring with its chill white breath
those silver-mirage days.

The Trans-sexual River

(for M.H.)

Yours was the convenient verbal sort —
just add an *e* and
see its hormones gel –

but I was surf-riding
a more muscular notion
of ladyboy water.

Sabrina I know well,
she who mutates twice-daily
when the moon bewitches her belly.

See her now,
ambling insouciantly between orchards,
swarthy, broad-shouldered,

carrying all before her
in a firm-hipped breast-stroke.
Just a touch of the Amazon here.

But catch her in her fighting gear,
arms flailing in a pumping crawl
as she heads the other way –

another sex entirely.
Rivers shouldn't do this,
not nice-well-bred-girl rivers.

This is headstrong, this is
indiscreet, this is
"Look at me, you guys."

He chucks logs, headbuts boats
against jetties, spouts
filthy gobs at watchers,

annexes sandbanks like a Viking,
snatches at saplings
to do his kung-fu fighting.

There's no living with Sabrinus
in his *getoutomyway* mode.
He goes as far as nature will endure

before he lies exhausted,
shoulders back against a weir
gazing up at the sky.

Watch now. It's happening.
Biceps shrink and liquefy,
dimpled breasts appear.

A mermaid with a tree-root for a tail
is reborn in that cross-gender vale
between Lower and Upper Parting.

"Forty Acres"

Framed by distant hills
silent rows of empty trucks
slice bars of sunlight.

Whirlwinds in the dust.
A breeze scorched by the foundry
picks the rust from wheels.

At one end, cobbles
glint in a brick-mouthed tunnel
where green water drips.

And here a footbridge
arched like an accordion
plays the air's lament.

Somewhere is the brook,
exhausted, cloaked by nettles,
ringed with iron reeds.

Where the bypass swoops,
a brown wreath of traffic fumes
clouds the lost Twyver.

Only rooted buffers
scorn the winds of change that blow
through Forty Acres.

Welcome Street

I

If once it fetched a grandeur from The Park,
it doesn't now,
and the Academy it was a tradesman's entrance for
has transferred to a green-field site
the other side of town.

Now it's just a backway to a car-park
or a nip-through spur off Friendly Street
with its hardware shop and Asian General Store.

Why should anybody come this way at all
but the curious, the lost?

Who is welcome now on Welcome Street?

II

Roman. Bishop. Bluecoat.
A city of sure foundations.
Everywhere around its ancient walls
they dig things up –
mosaics, mirrors, bones.

And now all men are archaeologists,
unearthing secrets long concealed
that wink in sudden light.
Things they might have owned, but dispossessed
in tidying their affairs
emerge with new-found pride.

A scapegoat has been found in Welcome Street.

III

One day the sun will slant again on Welcome Street.

And women, hurrying to the chip-shop
as they've done each week for years
with no stain on their minds but vinegar
and the latest catchy tune

And children, yes it's safe now,
will go scampering to The Park
or skipping in the shadow of a wall

Poor Jenny lies a-weeping

Sam Sam the dirty old man

Here comes a candle to light you to bed

Such quaint old songs.

Will these still be the songs they'll sing
when singing's welcome back on Welcome Street?

Ballad of The Beast

"Who slew the beast,
the still-untried beast?"
    "Not us," said the neighbours.
    "Despite his grim labours,
We'd not slay the beast."

"Who found the body,
the dangling-sack body?"
    "Me," said the warder,
    "obeying my orders,
I found the body."

"Who loosed the knot,
the well-practised knot?"
    "That was me too.
    What else could I do
but loosen the knot ?"

"Who kissed his lips,
his icy-blue lips?"
    "I," said the nurse,
    "for better or worse,
I kissed his lips."

"Who signed the book,
the heavy black book ?"
    "My job," said the clerk.
    "In the New Year's dark,
I signed the book."

"Who signed the cross,
the blood-token cross?"
    "I," said the priest,
    "though he's only a beast,
I signed the cross."

"Who's left to mourn?
What bereaved one must mourn?"
    "I must," said the wife,
    "though I sharpened the knife,
I'm left to mourn."

"Who heard his words,
his revealing last words?"
    "Me," said the son.
    "He denied what he'd done.
Those were his words."

"Who'll tell the people,
the clamouring people ?"
    "Let us," said The Press.
    "You clean up the mess
while we tell the people."

"Who'll read his will,
the beast's tainted will?"
    "Ahem," coughed the brief,
    "though it causes me grief,
There isn't a will."

"Who'll shovel the earth,
his close friend, the earth ?"
    "I will," said the son,
    "since I know how it's done,
I'll shovel the earth."

"Who'll dance on his grave,
his unmarked grave?"
    "We will," said the dead,
    " 'til the soil seeps red,
We'll dance on his grave."

"Who'll spell the blame,
the beast's untried blame?
    "Will you, balladeer?"
    "No blame. No fear.
I'll not mention his name."

Pay per view

See tomorrow's headlines today as they happen.
Click here *now.*

No automatic renewal or sudden hike in fees.
Pay only for what you see.

Today's special feature direct from Georgia,
brought to you by I-Ball .com.

Press the info tab to find how you can be there,
plus downloadable preview free.

On-screen in real time , two dollars per minute.
Leave when you wish with no penalty.

Register now through our secure server,
with payment by credit card.

Please enter a password of four to eight digits.
GLOAT has been taken. Please choose again.

See clips here from our top-selling videos,
courtesy of our sponsor, *FRANK.net.*

Ensure that no minors are present, then
Click Here for our gallery

That tabloids and do-gooders don't want you to witness.
Vote with your finger.

Enlarge any frame from our number one feature.
Please be patient . Don't exit yet.

Frame one : the first victim's family welcomed
by Governor Vince McGraw.

Frame two : the second victim's mother inspects
the hi-tec circuitry.

Frame three: the witnesses take their seats.
Click here now to see Frame Four,

"Fitting the cap", or click "*Enough*"
if you don't wish to view any more.

Please note, all clips are copyright
Of *FRANK.net* .
Infringement will invite the full rigour
of current U.S. law.

Fur flies

Fur flies.
The night's an arena
of catcalls and stampings.
Shapes, stalking and circling.

A thrown glove
loops like a bat,
a bait taken up.
Silver slices the night.

Its weaving dance
skims the shine off cobbles,
splinters the lamplight,
sets the stars a-spin.

The moon, haughty moll
holding aloft her trophy,
flings a scarf of cloud
across her shoulder.

Shadows converge
round a bundled coat.
Someone has broken
the kaleidoscope's gold.

A breeze sweeps its
fragments against walls.
Tattooing rain
thunders on the roof-tins.

Torches and shouts
flicker and echo
down alleys that open
like wounds in the flanks of the night.

The Black Pad

Gentle as a nurse, the officer
takes the lad's splayed fingers
and presses each in turn
on the black pad.

As each tell-tale whorl
is grained onto the paper,
the officer chats through the old routine,
laughs at the risk of ink
to his light-grey slacks and yellow tie.

Next, the mug-shot.
There's a bother with the battery
and then a dodgy tripod.
One flash blinds him. Another, to make sure.
They like to make an impression on the young.

This is a rite of passage he'll remember.
No longer a face in a crowd,
but filed, a focus for surveillance.
They hand him back the watch he'd been so proud of.
His late father's. At least they've kept it clean.

Chap in a balaclava?

"Who was the chap in the balaclava?"
You shake your head.
Is your furrowed look just another pretence
or pain provoked by the memory?
"On a bike. A mountain-bike. Red."

You can't help them on this one.
This is stick or bust.
Red, it must be a herring.
Blue lights you know all about.
Who can you trust?

And how did this chap come to exist
in the first place?
Did some nark's brainwave dream him up
and stick him there, a sinister watcher,
a figure with no face?

Could he be the phantom main-man
in a business nobody planned?
Was it him who grabbed you
as you mooched in the churchyard
and thrust that stuff in your hand?

Is there a chap-in-a-balaclava –
a shadow on the road,
keeping nookey, as much on you
as on the doorway, making sure you cough up
everything you owed?

Interrogation

It's been noted you never said sorry.
That would mean hearing them say
"Is that all you've got to say on the matter?"
"It's too late to be sorry now."
"Sorry is too small a word "
or "A word can't bring her back."
Did you want to say sorry?
You left me little else,
but it stuck like a fishbone in my throat.
Are you saying you did feel sorry?
Sorry, yes, that she didn't love me.
Sorry I'd got it wrong again again.
But sorry I touched her?
Never!
What about all the others?

Others? What others?
There were never others.
Never one like her.
Very well.
We'll talk again tomorrow.

Roll Call

In Memoriam Cecil Giddings *1899-1989*

You kept a propeller on the stairs,
Your brother's from the Great War, you said,
But I recognised that head for heights
When you lashed a ladder to the roof
At the age of 83.

Few of your generation made it
This far through the century
But the mourners filed
In sober print
The full length of the page.

Thank god for *"The Gazette."*
Else for how many months
Would I have scanned in vain
Through the pillars of the Market Hall
For your white hair or cap,

Or wondered if I'd half-an-hour to spare
To allay my guilt at not having called.
What a shock to learn
I'd missed the chance
Of a last malt by your coal-fire.

One summer, in the rose-arbour with Vera,
You lured me over the low brick-wall
To sip your elderberry brew;
And when my house of cards collapsed,
You took me in,

Your lodger in the garden-flat,
That den of wine and roses,
Your first married home,
Where I stewed and wrote of Ivor Gurney
And thought of your propeller on the stairs.

Now, two days before Remembrance,
Your return flight overdue,
Somewhere a crematorium chimney
Sputters into life.
No dogfight this.

School Boxing Match

(in memoriam Lyndon Morgan)

I'll never forget him –
one of my lads.
He was
a set-up :
thought he was taking on
someone with experience
and went in hard.
Soon eased off when he saw
his opponent's lack of guard.
"Sorry sir.
Are you all right ?"
A shaking of hands.

Four years later he left for Ulster.

A shaking of hands.
"Are you all right ?"
"Sorry sir."
His opponent's lack of guard
soon eased off. When he saw
and went in hard,
someone with experience
thought he was taking on
a set-up.
He was.

One of my lads…
I'll never forget him.

Still Talking to Bob

I think of you, Bob, wherever I walk round here.
Not just on your patch, but
in the town, the streets, the fields – everywhere.

Since that one-way trip, your sphere has spread,
extended like the shade
of a playground tree, as your wide frame did.

It drifts like a hot-tea fug in your Greasy Spoon,
or ambles towards me
with two plastic bags on a hot afternoon.

For you a race picked up at the final bend.
Now, in Maurice Ball's the Bookies,
over my shoulder : *"Not a chance, my friend."*

From the path through brambles below your site
your ghost on the skyline beckons
more than any memorial seat :

a bear, a tree, a slab of granite rock,
like your bulk in the doorway
after meetings, parties, waiting to lock up.

The autumn wind in the copper-beech could be
your jingling keys, your heavy sighs
pleading, *"Account for me."*

For Roger

I think you'd have welcomed the rebirth of the rain
this silver afternoon, trees humped beneath their shrouds,
the insubstantial distance, smouldering clouds,
this dwindling into winter once again.

You'd have sat here at the window, noting how
wet ball-bearings trickle down the bough
of the wrought-iron tree, and watching one lone crow
doggedly row home across the ria of the sky.

Before you left, shuffled towards the stairs,
not finishing that final frugal meal,
you closed your notebook, tacitly declared
you'd sat the show through once, and what was left to see
was a loop of film, like the seasons on a wheel,
the to-and-fro of tides in the starlit bay.

Questions

Why
should they die,
all those friends we hoped might live forever?
Who decides to sever
their lines across the widening river?

Where
do they bear
their swiftly-emptied haversack of hope?
Down what strange sunlit slope
do their shadows dwindle and lose shape?

When
if again
shall our smiles warm their time-whitened faces
except in those places
where ghosts linger, where our blood freezes?

What
remains that
can testify they ever walked here, keep -
sakes from the jumbled heap
of nothings in which they fell asleep?

These
images:
the phosphorescent flare of their spent days,
their words, their random ways
of loving, their momentary gaze.

Eleventh of November

The fog has cleared
and the countryside breathes again;
autumn trees on the hillside
are regiments of colour.

I stand with trowel and small fork,
ready now for winter.
It was a close thing.
The earth is churned.

shrivelled leaves and snapped stalks
lie at my feet,
but the scarlet geraniums
are safe from the frost.

They stand to attention
in their winter pots,
their medals glowing
in the afternoon light.

Across the rooftops,
along the ragged hedges,
the sound of a bugle
echoes from the town.

Environmental Health

Another funeral with only me to mourn
apart from a policeman, and the priest
who dandles life and death
three times a day, with water.

Someone goes down I thought I didn't know,
but here now, in the slicing rain
that patters on the coffin-lid
and glistens the yellow clay,
I seem to know her better than anyone
at this has-to-be-got-through ritual.

Each one takes time to get over :
a large mug of tea
or, as today, a whiskey.
Then those random dreams, months hence maybe,
of walking up carpetless stairs
in a dark of putrefaction.

We'll advertise as a matter of course,
legal patter in the local rag, the London Times,
in the hope of getting through
to some estranged one, some colleague who remembers
a chance remark, a phone-call
on an anniversary.

There's money in abundance,
under mattresses, in bureaux, a dozen bank accounts,
sufficient to buy that marble headstone
that no-one bothers to read but me.
All present and correct, sir.

At the gate, the undertaker
slips a little something in my hand.
Before I look I know what it will be.
A wedding ring.

It will be stored of course,
cross-referenced,
for the specified length of years,

We almost overlooked it.

Ash

(for Chris Collier)

"I am soft sift in an hour-glass" - *G.M. Hopkins*

It could be disheartening how the memory drifts,
like the stuff itself, winnowed on the air,
and neither its last location, nor crumbling embers
that clog the woodburner's grill.
recall promptly enough that bright morning when
we passed the jar from palm to palm
like a training-pitch ball,
one arm flung out like a sower's.

You can't after all spend a life
remembering – there are fires to be lit and
a game to be got through.

But every so often, when the sun sets ablaze the turf,
or when a wing-threequarter dives in triumph
on that hallowed space between fence and goal,
I sense him , hovering there, smugly satisfied
that the boys have twigged at last,

And I'm drawn to wondering – of that grey-flake talcum
that burrowed in the grass until the hoses turned on,
exactly what remains.

Homage to Eddie

You always were a cute kid,
and the way you blended licks
could have put you in the stratosphere with Spector.

But then again you might have quit, chilled out,
settled for fishing,
shrugged off those *Summertime Blues*.

As it was, you never went surfin',
never got stewed,
never changed your face to a spaced-out dude's.

Didn't know how much I dug you
until now, with this
double-fold vinyl on a market stall.

The *Cadillacs* are rusted out, or in museums.
Gaggias are *Starbucks*
and Drive-Thru's thicker on the ground than undertakers.

For more than forty years
Chippenham's been a pilgrim's patch
the fast route to Heathrow left for dead.

So why in Leek? Why surface here,
in an Easter market best for haggling
for hoes, dibbles, game-pie? Could this be *retro-chic*?

On the 30th Anniversary of Elvis Presley's death

Still dressed to kill in their crepes and drapes,
trapped in a Graceland grief for shellac rakes
who, tommy-gunned by drumrolls, spun a coin
then staggered to the glowing *Wurlitzer*
to punch their favourite number in the groin,
these cats and chicks, now pallid beneath glitter,
take up again the *hippy hippy shake*.

Thirty years since Elvis joined the Blest,
the rockers are all bopping to their rest.
Like Gunn's, my pen's obsessed with elegies
for friends in sweating beds with rotten breath,
haunted by their dreams of a young man's death,
borne to the stars on a jitterbugging breeze.

Homage to Stanley

(In Memoriam   Stanley Unwin)

Gobble is dead. Long may she liver .
Never his gabble so much on the radiophobe
As today, when silence stuff his cleft palate
With its black dentifrice.

All we utter thus when bakelite spuddle
Steamified and scorchy
Make of our tongue a fat Q.

Only Mikhail Bent-tin spake so weasel
To little papoose that we had to
Stuff our mouth with hankerchives.

Stanley. A monicker to conjurbole.
Not he of the jungle hi-de-hi
Or jolly Fat Boy Slim.
Could he have got titter with gobble
Has his label read Wayne
Or JCB Donoval?

I think not , seldom, never if sometime.
What's in a monicker, you ask,
A rosyglow by any other,
Pongsweet balcony kiss and such.
Ay, there's the rubicon.

And now from the gravyboat
We hear him everywhere.

All the speshy blandines of Mister Tony Blather,
All excuse why the price be wider,
The tramcar conky , the gasbill kerpow ,
All sing to the strain of his loop-ole solfa,
All smack of Stanley now.

Farewell O'Grady

Whisky and cigars, the smug tight skin
as we sank into cushions, faces hot
from the log-fire,
our babies undulating gently
several rooms away

When someone said,
"You know O'Grady's dead?"

There could be no doubt, there being
only one O'Grady,
but still I had to check :
*"Not the O'Grady,
he of the craggy face
and peremptory whistle?"*

It had been passed around for days,
this juicy morsel.
When the shock softened, they even risked a joke.

O'Grady was dead then.
It bore consideration.
A heart attack had drawn the sting
that novices would never fear again.

I thought of his striding
in badged and tight-buttoned blazer
on the hottest day of the year;
his killer forehand, his breadth
behind a rank of trophies,
The letters that shone against his frame :
O'Grady A.B.C. and X.Y.Z.

Now the pea in the whistle was split,
his tannoy disconnected.
In his carpeted lair with the door ajar
they are hoovering, removing,
pictures of O'Grady.

Do this, do that,
Do it this way, that way.
Nobody move until I say.

O'Grady breathes
"Amen."

After Hermione left ...

...things went to pieces.
The gaffer, hair suddenly grey,
walked on his knees to the mausoleum
at 8 and 8 precisely.

Tourists ceased to come.
Shops were closed by 3,
buckets and spades fading in the windows,
and no shoals brought their silver to the bay.

The refurbished bistro on the promenade,
nouveau chic like its sister- place in Putney,
now does bolognaise for the workers,
little else.

The rumour goes that she's not really dead,
but that's par for the course with martyrs,
just like Joe Grimes heard Elvis singing
"Old Shep" by the lake.

Will we get her out of our system
before the whole place dies?
Or will the crane-jibs move in soon,
sent with foreign money,
to build burger-bars and schooner-shaped hotels,
and turn us all into theme-park guides,
presenting Royal waxworks
as if they were alive?

Beyond The Door

The absence of front doors

We live in a flat with no front door. It's awkward.
Like the farmhouse in "Cold Comfort Farm."
Our access is an iron fire-escape
that leads from our kitchen to the Harbour Master's Office.
Or we ride the dumb waiter
to the fitting rooms of "Jasmine's Lingerie"
who rent the shop below us in high season.

When Jasmine is hectic, I make a rope of sheets
and abseil onto the ice-cream parlour porch.
From there to the street is an ankle-jarring jump.
It injured me once, but it's a quick way down.
The only trouble is getting back up.

There's a skylight in the attic
where I sit and watch the clouds, seagulls, constellations,
and a local aircraft unrippling banners :
Vote for Lewis;
Clearance Sale at Megan's;
Disco at Borth Rygby Clyb Tonite.

But mainly I stay in and watch the telly —
old movies, makeovers, highlights from the Irish Shinty
League, while Sis knits balaclavas
for our boys in Kuala Lumpur
and auntie picks her corns.
Street life is ours only as a goldfish view.
The others seem to manage pretty well
but I feel like the Lady of Shallott.

Once I saw someone who looked like my mother
withdrawing what seemed like bars of gold
from the cash machine by the butcher's.
My frantic tapping broke the pane
and when glass showered down to the pavement,
she was off,
skittering in her high heels up the cobbled alley
past the Old Tudor Sex Shop.

Perhaps she thought it was someone shooting;
she was never one to get involved.
I think of that day often -
how it could have changed my life.
Perhaps it wasn't her. Or perhaps it was
and she knew that I was up there.
Perhaps - and this is the scariest thing –
what she was running from was me.

Ghost Walk

Couldn't find him anywhere —
as if I were starting at the wrong end.
Over ten years the town had put on weight
and seemed to face the other way.
But this was the place.
The striped lighthouse clinched it.

The Outfitters' I'd known him from was gone,
stripped down to a Pizza Shack, and a slot-machine arcade,
while the barber's where he'd sat for his Halloween trim
was a Starbuck's now.

Perhaps I'd catch him unawares at night,
gazing into the green-floored harbour,
or at morning with his tripod on the cliff-path,
when the bay was a shoal of light.

Then I saw the poster for "The Ghost Walk."
 "Meet here at eight," it said.
I thought it worth the salty anecdotes
of one-eyed sailors, gliding Caldey monks,
worth traipsing endless iron fire-escapes
to upper rooms with no front doors,
to catch a glimpse of him.

For a moment, by the churchyard lamp,
I thought he was our guide.
Night's sleight-of-hand again.
For, no, his name was Burnside
and he'd moved down here from Edgeware
when his sister died.

Was it his silhouette I saw,
threading the five stone arches?
Was his voice one of those raised in raucous song
in the Lifeboatman's Arms?

I thought walled towns sealed all our memories in
just as all our words go round and round the cosmos
till the end of what's called Time.

But now I'll have to sleep with Doubt.

It was a good week in many ways, but not what I came for.
Times and people change. I shan't come back.

Horreos

Garden-sheds with granite crosses
line the Sanxenxo shore
like ostentatious charabancs
or nabobs' bathing-huts.

But down Gallegan lanes,
inland from the twisting rias,
they're foundered high and dry
like remnants of some flood.

Petrified arks, granary landships
from which the rats have never leapt,
they perch on mushroom staddlestones,
bearing their crosses like kings.

Breezes vamp their hobo harmonica slats,
nudge haywisps under musty sacks.
If I could float one back, I'd have it
for a writing-shed, a lupin-high gazebo.

I'd pull up its drawbridge ladder
and sit, legs dangling, on its parapet,
watching the buzzards wheel above Stinchcombe,
monarch of all I survey,

while behind me in the cobwebbed dark,
my cargo of pears and flagons of Rioja
would strengthen my heart for the voyage ahead
through the sea-frets of winter.

Hostages to Fortune

We bought 'em in Lanjaron, caked with Alpujarra soil,
and one night, when the wind whipped cold,
they were coddled in foil
and given up to the furnace of the woodstove
which crackled and swore,
consuming the cones and kindling
we had hammocked in a Barbour
from the Parc Natural.

The foil couldn't take it –
shrivelled and disintegrated,
blackening their skins like a martyr's helpless hands,
But their integrity remained,
hearts hard as a heretic's
sizzled as we thrust the spike in –
such are the spuds of the Alpujarras.

When the wine was down to dregs
we had them for supper,
puckered from the microwaves.
They crumbled then,
luscious as roasted chestnuts
and sparked all night
our smoke-and spark-filled dreams.

From a Bangkok Boarding House Noticeboard

Beware gem scams.
If a taxidriver tells you
there's a special taxfree week on gems
do not go with him.

Keep your moneybelt with you all the time .
No-one rides for free.

Beware of tuk-tuk driver 5235 .
He beat me and took all my cash.

Rafe, I opted to move down the road
for air-conditioning.
Suk Pasath Guest House,
Soi Mai Rong.
See you there. Jess. Wednesday.

Spare an hour to call
on James Callander
an old Scottish guy serving 50 years.
Take the Chao Praya riverboat to Nonthaburi
Then 1st left, 1st right.
He doesn't get many visitors.

Cockerels among cabins

The Thai is trailing
two cockerels through the cabins
up from the sea.
He's gravy-brown.
The leading bird is black.
It scurries as a thin-boned adolescent
would waddle with his surfboard —
all limbs and shiver.

The second is a ladyboy.
He high-steps, craning his neck
to acknowledge the crowd —
a scrawny Queen-Mother,
his plumage tailored in the Silom Road,
a jockey in his silks.

Where are they heading ?

Between junked folding chairs
of defunct restaurants,
between the wooden piles
of beach-bum bungalows ,
past steaming woks, the leaky hose,
and tree-stumps like amputated Buddhas,
past blotches of mimosa

towards the shadow of the wood
in the foetid afternoon
over grit and grot
through rut and root
go the two black cocks
and the lithe brown Thai
with his smoking cigarette
in a pre-monsoon procession.

Shelley

I saw you, Shelley, but you didn't see me,
leaning over the balcony
of a Bangkok whorehouse
where lurid lights flashed on and off
the proffered flesh of midriffs
and a seductress wailed in stereo
above the clash of Thai Grunge.

I longed to call up, to hear your *"Hi!"*
in those rich round Bristol tones,
but a firetruck passed, then a tuk-tuk
and I let the moment by.

But then I'm glad I did.
You'd only have offered a discount massage
when I was running with sweat
and obsessed with dysentery.

How could I humiliate you thus,
let you know I'd seen you,
the day before I flew back home,
your hair bundled at the nape
like it always was at school,
and the white lace of your shoulder-straps
stained a khaki-grey.

Three flies

Into the ashtray drops the fly,
a dead black husk, like a rabbit's pellet,
that has lain on the ledge since I smacked it.

It seemed until now too small a thing
to take trouble with –
fetching a page to flick it in the bin.
But having at hand this dish of crushed stubs
it seems fit to cremate it
with the glowing end of my small cigar.

And even as it sizzles and is gone,
reminding me of Mother, Mike and John,
another fly is crawling up the pane
dazzled by the bright air it seeks,
knowing nothing of incineration, nothing of
my half-explained urge for its extinction.

But I let it be, am snared instead
by its intricate fragility
as I watch its hair-fine legs go zithering up,
its silver wings, like a fairy's, all atwitch,
its plump body bristling with desire.

It pirouettes and loops the loop to a curtain.
Perhaps it has seen through the glass
with its pinhead eyes
another of its kind being winnowed by the breeze
on the gibbet of a spider's web.

Last Fly

(for Eunice and Alan Musk)

I am sent to demolish
the last fly on earth
with my rolled-up
frayed and blood-streaked
TLS.
I have tracked him down
to this last square room.

The kitchens of all my friends
are peppered with corpses,
squashed currants,
smeared pulp,
fractured diaphanous wings,
and for months I have learned
to stalk each flick,
my shots echoing like gunfire.

Once and for good,
heedless of ecologists' pleas,
I shall rid the earth of flies.
I don't give a damn for fishermen,
those sedentary golfers
with maggots in tubs.

The irksome crawlers
that tickled the hairs on my legs
and darkened the eyes of donkeys
as they stood mournful in buzzing meadows
have finally had their day.

Only one left already.
There he is
on the bureau by the wineglass,
playing his cunning game,
safe, as he thinks,
among sacred fragile things.

How wrong he is.
I am the Flykiller General.
When he makes his move for the door jamb
I shall be there.

WHAPP!
I live only for the moment
when the last fly is dead.

Last glimpse

The season is dying.
A hint of light catches
the pigeons' final flourish
as you look up
above the dressed-stone frontage.

Workers and students scurry out of
the encroaching twilight
all the way up
the station approach.

Neon already etches
its graffiti on the city.

Only a month ago
I lingered and marvelled
at sunset's pink flush
on Brunel's masterpiece.

Now monochrome is setting in,
the evening a fading print
and soon no-one will believe in
September's gilding.

Across a month, much changes.
Later I'll see the moon,
its cape across one shoulder,
shiver in the Avon.

Not long now before I hurry in
from afternoons whose flare
is skin-deep only,
to the solace of crackling wood
and hot sweet tea.

Here the buses' doors release
those who weren't around to see
the century change shape,
whose clothes I cannot figure,
whose language is a patois.

This Moment

This, for the moment, is where I'm glad to be,
waiting for the heron to appear;
at my viewing-place above the estuary
in the last burning sunlight of the year.
The wind is flexing silver like a blade;
the leaves are tinder, brittle, red and dry.
But in this coombe the hand of time is stayed,
unmoving as the clouds in a frost-blue sky.

On a muddy shore, half-lost through boughs and bracken,
the masts of boats strike white against the hill.
In ebbing pools their weed-draped lines have slackened,
freed awhile from the drag of the current's will.
Late afternoon, I know, the sun will slide,
abandon this bay to a chopping, chafing tide.

"A Final Word from our Leader"

To John Pritchard

So we've made it to the end of another long semester.
A hard one I'm sure for subject and abject.
Thank you for your effervescence, your professional
whatever.
It's had its ups – I cite but one example :
the number going on to Honours Etymology.
There have of course been more.
But every institution as plethoric as ours
must inevitably take its share
of the Ultimate Valediction.
I call for one minute's silence
for those who've gone before.

Thank you.
Which brings me to the Fritillary Awards.
Mrs Fritillary was here before the Building.
In her bequest she made provision.
Will this year's winners step up now
to possess their luminous scrolls
and curtsey to her bust.

Sadly we always say goodbye to someone
bound for postures new.
Unity Postlip has been at Frazzled Heath
more years than most of us care to remember,
first as Head of Hair,
and latterly as i/c Fingers.
She takes with us our best etceteras for the sometime,
and hopes you will join her in a celebratory tot
(which should explain the enigmatic phrase
in the End of Semester arrangements).

It only remains for me to wish
and blow the candles out,
hoping you come back like fighting lions
when the Car Park's been redone.

The Leader

Sometimes half his instructions pass them by –
how long it'll take, the time to come back.
If only the leader put it down in black
and white, not just for the ear but for the eye.
Sometimes they hear but have no wish to comply,
prefer to do their own thing – not that they lack
respect for his aims, but they want to attack
with blood-curdling shout, not loin-girding sigh.

Some walk out on him early, already fired
with vision, excitement, the key to the vault,
deep, well before they leave, in dreams of desire.
If they don't do it his way, is it his fault?
It was just that once, they caught him lying,
supplying sugar, claiming it was salt.

Déjà vu

"This is where we came in…"
they say,
and creak their seats to go.

A bus to catch, maybe,
a need for air,
or just the sweat
of living it through again.

Blest are those who come
when the schedules say.
They see it clear.
They leave in light.

The children always want to stay,
"to see that good bit when…"
How they relish its approach !

And some who always stay,
lacking a place to go;
those who choose snug dark for sleep;
the simple who don't recognise the seams.

If we could train ourselves
to sit it out,
to will the déjà vu,
perhaps we'd spy the hero's doubt,
the make-up on the frontage,
or amazingly a sequence
we'd somehow missed before.

For where we came in
is an illusion,
a trick of the eyes
adjusting to the dark.